THIS BOOK BELONGS TO:

I AM A GIRL I CAN BE ANYTHING!

I AM BEAUTIFUL

I CAN BE A FASHION MODEL

I AM STRONG

I CAN BE A SPORTS STAR

I AM UNSTOPPABLE

I CAN BE A RACING DRIVER

I AM IMPORTANT

I CAN BE A POLICE OFFICER

I AM CONFIDENT

I CAN BE A SINGER

I AM PATIENT

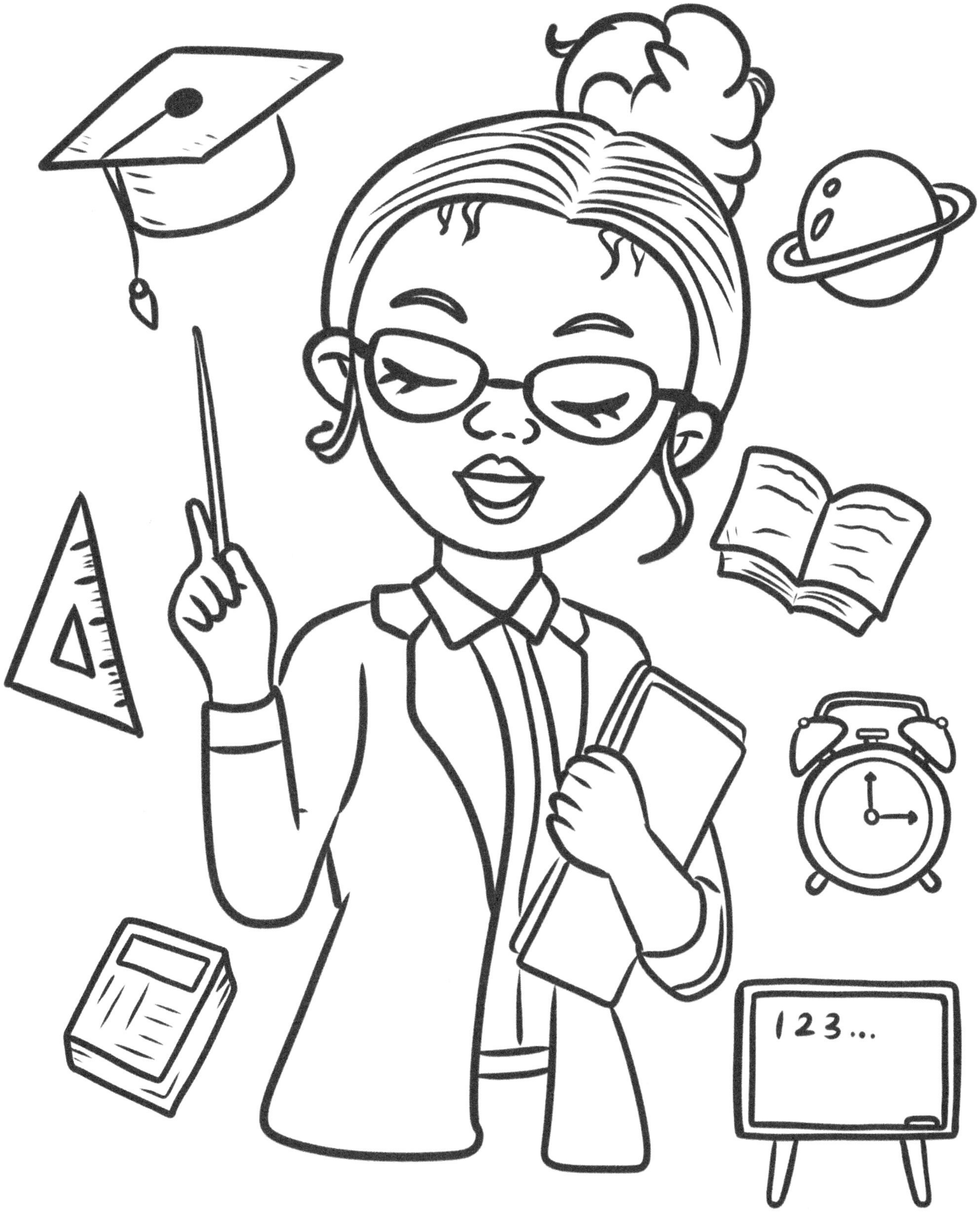

I CAN BE A TEACHER

I AM RESPONSIBLE

I CAN BE A JUDGE

I AM AMBITIOUS

I CAN BE A MILITARY OFFICER

I AM PASSIONATE

I CAN BE A CHEERLEADER

I AM FRIENDLY

I HAVE WONDERFUL FRIENDS

IMAGINE YOUR BRIGHT FUTURE!

CAN YOU CONNECT
THE DOTS?

CAN YOU CONNECT THE DOTS?

CAN YOU CONNECT THE DOTS?

CAN YOU CONNECT THE DOTS?

MAZE CHALLENGE

MAZE CHALLENGE

MAZE CHALLENGE

CAN YOU COLOR BY NUMBERS?

1.BLUE   2.RED   3.YELLOW   4.ORANGE
5.BROWN   6.GREEN   7.GREY

CAN YOU COLOR BY NUMBERS?

1.BROWN   2.RED   3.YELLOW   4.ORANGE
5.GREEN   6.DARK GREEN   7.PINK

CAN YOU COLOR BY NUMBERS?

1.PINK   2.RED   3.PURPLE   4.ORANGE
5.YELLOW   6.GREEN   7.BROWN   8.GREY

Find 3 Differences Between The 2 Pictures

Find 3 Differences Between The 2 Pictures

Find 3 Differences Between The 2 Pictures

Match The Professions With Their Names

TEACHER

ASTRONAUT

CHEF

FIREFIGHTER

Match The Items With Their Names

SUN

UNICORN

ICECREAM

RAINBOW

SPACESHIP

Match The Animals With Their Names

BIRD

ELEPHANT

DEER

DOLPHIN

KOALA

Match The Items
With Their Names

HAT

HIGH HEELS

BAG

TROUSERS

SKIRT

Word Search Career

Can you find the words hidden in the puzzle?

```
S  E  A  S  T  E  A  C  H  E  R  C
C  E  E  E  A  G  O  A  A  N  T  A
S  H  H  C  S  G  A  A  R  C  R  G
F  P  O  C  T  S  T  C  R  L  A  R
B  T  P  C  R  I  Q  M  O  E  J  A
U  H  S  H  O  I  A  Q  T  R  U  N
N  P  I  A  N  I  S  T  P  R  D  L
N  R  N  T  A  N  H  X  N  T  G  M
Y  V  B  A  U  K  E  T  C  H  E  F
P  W  R  I  T  E  R  S  E  E  R  H
A  H  O  L  I  D  A  Y  G  R  R  E
S  H  U  S  T  H  T  E  H  U  N  T
```

CHEF　　　**ASTRONAUT**

PIANIST　　**JUDGE**

WRITER　　**TEACHER**

Word Search Inspiration

Can you find the words hidden in the puzzle?

```
C S N U R A I N B O W D
F N L P M H K O R T U P
B E A U T I F U L I R A
O W A O L A R B E E I T
W B Y R O S F N Z D C I
E E G U L F O C E I K E
R L B R S E T R U S C N
S L D B O K S I A G A T
R R P R M W E S M A R T
S T R O N G S T O R I S
D F C O N F O V L U N N
A S B U T T E R F L G E
```

CARING

SMART

STRONG

BEAUTIFUL

PATIENT

FEARLESS

Word Search Animal

Can you find the words hidden in the puzzle?

```
R E D Y C N E B U N D B
A L A A S E I L M P U U
I E I T E S S A B I A T
N P S C P T Q D R C P T
C H Y W K A U D E N A E
O A N I P N I F L I R R
A N T S E E R T L C T F
T T L I P A R A A N Y L
Y O S U H B E A R I S Y
R A I N B I L T S H I H
G F I C H R O I T Y A U
B L O S S D O G B U G G
```

KITTY   BIRD

DOG   SQUIRREL

ELEPHANT BEAR

Word Search
Solutions

Career

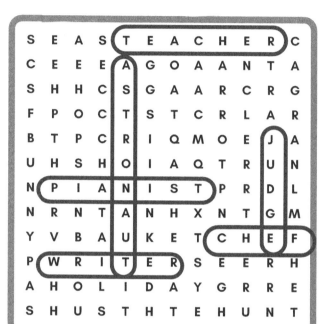

S	E	A	S	T	E	A	C	H	E	R	C
C	E	E	E	A	G	O	A	A	N	T	A
S	H	H	C	S	G	A	A	R	C	R	G
F	P	O	C	T	S	T	C	R	L	A	R
B	T	P	C	R	I	Q	M	O	E	J	A
U	H	S	H	O	I	A	Q	T	R	U	N
N	P	I	A	N	I	S	T	P	R	D	L
N	R	N	T	A	N	H	X	N	T	G	M
Y	V	B	A	U	K	E	T	C	H	E	F
P	W	R	I	T	E	R	S	E	E	R	H
A	H	O	L	I	D	A	Y	G	R	R	E
S	H	U	S	T	H	T	E	H	U	N	T

Inspiration

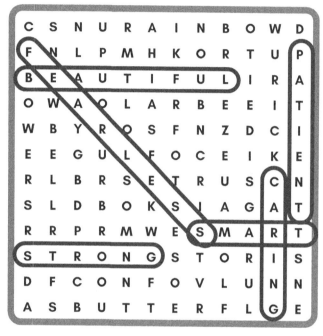

C	S	N	U	R	A	I	N	B	O	W	D
F	N	L	P	M	H	K	O	R	T	U	P
B	E	A	U	T	I	F	U	L	I	R	A
O	W	A	O	L	A	R	B	E	E	I	T
W	B	Y	R	O	S	F	N	Z	D	C	I
E	E	G	U	L	F	O	C	E	I	K	E
R	L	B	R	S	E	T	R	U	S	C	N
S	L	D	B	O	K	S	I	A	G	A	T
R	R	P	R	M	W	E	S	M	A	R	T
S	T	R	O	N	G	S	T	O	R	I	S
D	F	C	O	N	F	O	V	L	U	N	N
A	S	B	U	T	T	E	R	F	L	E	E

Animal

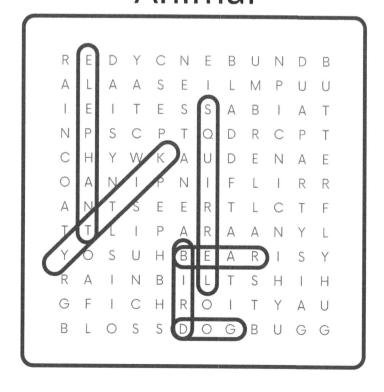

R	E	D	Y	C	N	E	B	U	N	D	B
A	L	A	A	S	E	I	L	M	P	U	U
I	E	I	T	E	S	S	A	B	I	A	T
N	P	S	C	P	T	Q	D	R	C	P	T
C	H	Y	W	K	A	U	D	E	N	A	E
O	A	I	P	N	I	F	L	I	R	R	R
A	N	T	S	E	E	R	T	L	C	T	F
T	T	L	I	P	A	R	A	A	N	Y	L
Y	O	S	U	H	B	E	A	R	I	S	Y
R	A	I	N	B	I	L	T	S	H	I	H
G	F	I	C	H	R	O	I	T	Y	A	U
B	L	O	S	S	D	O	G	B	U	G	G

Your Child's Joy, Our Purpose!

Dear Parents,

We appreciate your choice of our book for your child. Crafted with love, it's designed to spark creativity and learning.

As parents ourselves, we understand the impact of quality learning tools. We hope your child enjoys every moment with our book. Your feedback is vital. Please share your thoughts in a review.

Thank you for letting us be a part of your child's journey.

Warm regards,

WONDER POLLY

Made in the USA
Las Vegas, NV
23 December 2024

15326951R00063